A Beginner's Guide to Artificial Intelligence
For Boomers and Boards

By Brian Garr

Note: Unless noted otherwise, all pictures are by Unknown Author and are in public domain

FORWARD

was teaching a class on technology to a bunch of Credit Union board members in Palm Springs, California, and it seemed the most interactive part of the class was when we got to "what is artificial intelligence, and why should they care". These people, for the most part, were boomers, or older, and still remember rotary dialing. Once they got the fundamentals down, their inquisitiveness and exhilaration were contagious. That was when I realized that there are lots of folks out there, primarily boomers and older, that just get bombarded with buzz words and gobbledygook meant to make AI sound complex and difficult. Building artificial intelligence is most definitely complex and difficult but understanding how and why it works is not. So, I've written this book in the hopes of making artificial intelligence, and all of the hopes and frustrations around it, more understandable. This book is for those of us that refuse to say "Computer, set an alarm for eight am tomorrow". It's for those of us that really like that flip phone on TV with the really large buttons, because I don't want to order pizza on my phone, I want to call my kids. For this generation, our first exposure to smart computers was "HAL", the on-board computer from <u>2001 A Space Odyssey</u>. You just talked to HAL, like you might talk to your neighbor when asking for a cup of sugar. *"HAL, open the pod bay doors."* And like a spoiled adolescent, HAL responds *"I'm sorry, Dave. I'm afraid I can't do that."* So, some fifty years later, why do we have to ask computers to do things in a certain word order, or why doesn't it understand me half the time? Do computers really learn? What's deep learning, vs just plain old learning? What's neural about a computer network? All these questions, and more, will be answered in the pages that follow. I've spent the better part of my life delivering presentations on technology to people that don't understand technology, so my hope is that, with this book, I can bring a little enlightenment, and a little education, in a non-threatening way, to my generation, and my parent's generation, about artificial intelligence. AI is called an emerging technology because it's not ripe yet. It makes mistakes. Artificial Intelligence has been a lab project since the early 1950s, and it is still in its infancy. Using computers to translate one spoken language to another spoken language is still not quite good enough, and it's been around for over 50 years as well. So I hope that after reading this book, you will be able to understand what AI is, and what you can expect in the short term, and in the long term. Each chapter represents some flavor of AI, and I've intentionally kept each chapter short, so that no one AI concept becomes laborious or boring. The folks who write mystery novels and novels about the Singularity get to spin fanciful fictional stories about AI and what it will become. What I've tried to do here is spin short explanations of how AI works for us in everyday life, and where it is going in the near future. If you are a business executive who doesn't need to build AI, but would like to understand it, or if you are a hobbyist who just wants to know what's going on with AI, then I've written this book for you. Enjoy!

TACKLING ARTIFICIAL INTELLIGENCE

The term Artificial Intelligence, AI for short, is bandied about quite liberally in everyday discourse. "My son's doing incredible things bringing AI to Moe's Diner", translation: He's yelling out "Alexa, set a timer for 30 minutes" when starting a meatloaf. Or "I've trained my personal AI to turn on all the lights in my house", translation: I bought some new light bulbs from GE that somehow talk to my Google Home device.

AI has been around in the lab for as long as there have been computers. To give you an idea of some of the history of AI, the first well known AI conference was held in the 1950's at Dartmouth College, with the intent of writing down a working definition for AI and how to achieve the goal of creating the technology to match the definition. At the time, the goal was to be able to mimic the way humans learn, so the goal was to be able to solve problems that only the human brain could solve. As time progressed, AI became a subject of great investment, and then, after disappointment, disinvestment. These downturns in investment are called "AI Winter". For example, in the late 1970's scientists at MIT created a new programming language called LISP, specifically designed for developing AI applications, and created LISP machines that were powerful enough to run and compile LISP applications. A few of these scientists left MIT and created LISP Machines, Inc. These LISP machines were very powerful, but, as we have seen again and again with computers, next year's computers are twice as powerful as today's computers. Such was the nature of the computer industry, and, to much degree, still is. It wasn't long before regular IBM PCs were as powerful, if not more powerful, than the LISP machines. That was only one of many reasons that it wasn't long before LISP and LISP Machines, Inc, went out of business. After making huge bets on LISP, it was only natural that investors didn't want to put any more money into AI anytime soon. This was the trigger for one of many AI Winters over the past 70 years. If you want to sound really smart and apocryphal in front of your peers, or, more importantly, your kids, just say something like "I fear there is another AI Winter coming, and it's going to be a cold one".

Artificial Intelligence is an umbrella that covers many technologies that we use every day. Speech

Recognition, where your spoken words are turned into text, is AI. So is natural language understanding, which 'understands' those text words and responds accordingly. I know that may be confusing, so let me go over that again, because many people I meet think that Speech Recognition IS Natural Language Understanding. It is not. There are actually two different AI engines used when you tell a computer to do something and it does it. First, there is Speech Recognition, which takes your voice, and turns it into text. That capability is used for many different solutions, such as converting someone talking into closed captions, or for dictating a letter using your voice. Many doctors use a speech recognition program to turn their dictation into text, for their patient records. Speech recognition is the first half of what a device like Alexa™ does. Then the natural language understanding technology takes that text that was created from your voice and decides what your intent was. "Turn on the hall lights" is the intent to have the computer turn on the hall lights. Sometimes the intent is more complex. "What's the weather today?", is the intent to find out what today's weather is, but to get that answer, the computer has to determine your location, and then go to the internet to a weather reporting engine, ask it for the weather for your location, and then interpret the output of the weather engine so that it can report back the weather to you in an easily understandable dialog. It's a lot of work that happens in milliseconds, but all you really want to know is, "what's the weather?"

For future reference, in this book I talk a lot about an "AI Engine". The AI engine does this or does that. The most common architecture for AI is to create an engine that has a specific use. The engine is not a physical engine, but it runs on a physical computer as a software program. That software program is always running waiting for a question, so that it can work on the answer, and output a final answer after doing some work. Quite often you will see the terms "webservice", and "API" to describe the input and output from this AI engine. Even though we can't visit the webservice on the internet and see a web page, the webservice is still there, and the API, which stands for Application Programming Interface, is the method by which we ask questions and return answers. The diagram below shows a typical architecture for a request coming from personal assistant product that you may have in your home.

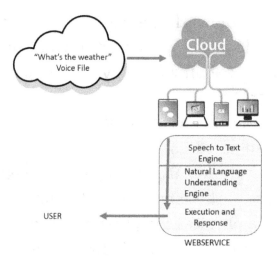

1. Voice File gets sent to the AI cloud platform
2. Speech to Text engine turns voice into text
3. NLU engine determines the intent of the text
4. Execution logic finds and formats the answer
5. Sends the answer back to the user

The user asks their AI device for a weather report. The device records the user's voice and sends that sound file to the cloud where the device's backend lives. There, the sequence of events is for the backend server to recognize that a request is coming in, then send it to the appropriate AI engines. In our example, the sound file is first sent to an AI engine that turns spoken words into text. Once the words are translated into text, the text is then sent to an AI engine which determines the meaning, or intent, of the text. In our example, the intent is go get the weather report. Next the intent is sent to a program that knows where to go to get the weather report, gets it, and then formats it in a way that is considered palatable for the user, and then sends the result to the user.

Machine Translation is another kind of AI technology that turns text from one human language to another. So is the scanner that turns your photo of written words into written words that can be manipulated in a text editing application, such as Microsoft Word™. The part of your camera that senses where someone's face is, and focuses there, is AI. There are lots more examples, but the one thing that all AI has in common is that it has an error rate. That's right, no technology that is truly AI is perfect. It always has a demonstrable error rate. An example: Let's say that we want all those security cameras around our house to recognize when a human is approaching, but we don't want it to beep at us when it is an animal. To start, we have to train our AI engine on what a human looks like. Well, it usually has two legs, walks upright, has two arms, and the human body has a normal leg to chest to head measurement relationship. The key word is "usual", because we know that there will be humans approaching our house that are not "usual", and I don't mean in the crazy relative way. Maybe they have only one arm, or use a wheelchair, or don't have the normal measurement relationships between their body parts. Ok, so we use training data in the form of pictures of thousands, or millions of humans, to train the engine on what humans look like. Then, to be sure that we help the engine as much as possible, we also train the engine to recognize the most common animals one might see, such as a squirrel, a deer, maybe a bear. Since there is almost an infinite number of possible silhouettes that our engine may have to recognize, we can't possibly find data to cover all the possibilities. Thus, instead of just saying "yes", or "no" to the hypothesis "this is a human", we get a confidence score. "There is an 87% confidence that this is a human." Then engine can never be 100% confident, because that would mean that the engine is only trained to recognize one particular figure, and would give false negatives on all other humans.

Let's apply that same definition to something as complex as speech recognition, the ability to turn your spoken words into text. There are an infinite combination of words and word senses that can be made into sentences. The English language is remarkably ambiguous. You can't really "crack a joke". You can crack an egg, but a joke? Because there are an infinite number of possible word combinations that form sentences, no matter how many actual sentences we use for training data, it will never be more than a fraction of all possible sentences and senses. Thus, we know that a speech recognition AI engine is going to have an error rate.

With the knowledge that AI, by definition, has an error rate, let's look at a couple of the most frustrating AI issues that the public runs into.

NEURAL NETWORKS AND DEEP LEARNING

The most difficult concept that you will need to learn to fully enjoy this book, is the concept of Neural Networks or Neural Nets, for short. Don't freak out, because this is really easy to understand. Those of us in the technology business took our early ques from the medical industry and just made everything sound and look incredibly complicated so that we would have job security. You can learn this, because it's really very simple. Below is the most common graphic used to show graphically a neural network engine. We use the term engine because it contains all the parts to work.

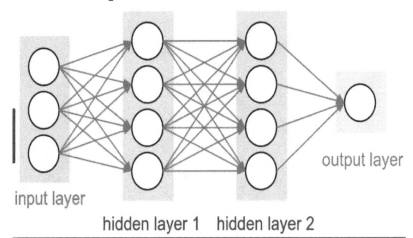

input layer

hidden layer 1   hidden layer 2

output layer

Other than being an impressive visual of lots of circles, and lots of connecting lines, what are we to make of this diagram. Well, input layer is obvious. We are going to input something, along with a guess (hypothesis), for example "I hypothesize that this picture is a picture of a cow." In AI terminology, we send the picture of the supposed cow to the engine. Now that picture is going to go through several hidden layers. Hidden layers? Why are they hidden? What are they hiding? Well, they are called hidden layers because we aren't quite sure what the system is finding or even how it is finding "things" in these hidden layers. It's true. Neural net developers have options of several existing algorithms, or they might invent their own algorithms to go into those hidden layers, but they don't have visibility into what is going on inside these hidden layers. We do know, in this example, that while training the engine, it looked at thousands, or maybe millions of pictures of cows, and it found tons of similarities, or patterns in these pictures. For example, it probably found that all cows have ears, nose, and mouth. Those are the easy ones, but it also founds all sorts of patterns that we might not find so evident. It uses these patterns to create rules about what a cow looks like so that it can identify a cow in the future. You can have as many hidden layers as you want in your engine, and each hidden layer has the job of either increasing or decreasing the confidence score of our hypothesis, because at the end of the process, the output layer, the engine is going to tell us the final confidence score on our hypothesis. Perhaps the picture really was of a cow, but with one leg missing. The confidence score may come back as 97% confidence that the picture was of a cow. Maybe we fed in a picture of a goat. The confidence score may come back with only a 4% confidence that the picture is a cow. The engine does not determine or suggest how you interpret these results. That is the job of the application developer, or, perhaps, you, the end user. If you get a 97% confidence score that the picture is of a cow, will you accept that the picture is of a cow? What about at 83%, or 45%?

For instructional purposes, let's say that we have a problem that we want to solve. The problem is that the number and types of roses in the world keeps growing as horticulturists, including hobbyists, keep creating new varieties of roses by splicing different kinds of roses together. We want to build an engine that can scan a picture of a flower and come back with a confidence score that it is a rose. We've decided amongst ourselves that a confidence score above 90% means it <u>is</u> a rose variant, between 50% and 90% confident means that it <u>may be</u> a rose, and below 50%

that it is <u>not</u> a rose. First, we need to go out and get some training data so that we can train our engine to understand what a rose looks like. Let's say we manually go out and get pictures of one thousand roses. We scan in all one thousand roses and split them into two groups, training data, and test data. In addition, we scan in 200 pictures of flowers that are not roses, so that we can test positive and negative recognition.

Training Data = 800 pictures of roses
Test Data = 200 pictures of roses plus 200 pictures of flowers that are not roses

For training, we send through our neural net rose detection engine the 800 actual pictures of roses, letting the engine know that the confidence score on these photos is 100%. Those hidden layers will find all sorts of patterns and markers in the rose pictures to create a list of what to look for to determine if a picture is a rose. This is the part, inside the hidden layers that we really don't know. But it happens. Inside the hidden layers, for example, the engine may find 400 different markers, or more, that raise the confidence that the picture is a rose. Now that we have done our initial training, we send through the 400 pictures of test pictures, of which 200 are of roses, and 200 are of non-roses. As it computes a confidence score for each picture, the developer of the engine gives feedback, both negative and positive, to the engine. The developer also has the opportunity to tweak or change the algorithms used in the hidden layers until they see the kind of confidence scores that they deem appropriate for the engine's task. Now here is the interesting part. If we train the engine to be 100% accurate on the training pictures, meaning it gets 100% confidence on all of the rose pictures, and 0% confidence on the non-rose pictures, then we have over-trained the engine to be perfect only on the training and testing set. Theoretically, this means that if a new rose is invented, one whose picture was not represented in the training and testing set, then the engine may not have a high confidence that it is a picture of a rose. Instead, what the developer is looking for is a high 90s percent confidence on pictures that are roses, and a low percent confidence score on pictures that are not of roses. With those results, we can feel confident that new varieties of roses will correctly have high confidence scores when sent through our engine. We can also say that one of the definitions of AI is a technology that always has some error rate.   Even before neural nets, AI always had an error rate. Whether we are talking about speech recognition, machine translation, picture identification, fingerprint matching. or even iris identification (considered the best biometric match of all), there is a measurable error rate. Last thought; if we were really creating this engine, we would use thousands, or tens of thousands of pictures for training.

WHY DOESN'T "ALEXA™" UNDERSTAND ME?

Ok, it's not just Alexa™. Whether you have Google Home™, Amazon Alexa™, Apple Siri™, or any of the other Personal Assistants, you've run into the issue where you ask what you think is a simple question "Who won the Cardinals game last night?", and you get an answer about Chicago hockey. Or you give your personal assistant an order "Turn off hallway lights", and it gives you back "I'm sorry, I didn't understand that". As we've already noted, there are actually two, or more, different AI engines involved in responding to your requests. The first step is to turn your speech into text. Speech recognition, which is the science of turning spoken words into text words, has an error rate. For simplicity sake, let's define your spoken question, or command, as an utterance. Your utterance doesn't have to be a full sentence, and it could only be one word long, such as "stop". But, for purposes of this conversation, let's agree that what came out of your mouth is called an utterance. To turn your utterance into text, there are lots of factors that go into the accuracy of the resultant text, such as your accent, the amount of background noise, and the vocabulary of your utterance. Like any AI engine, the speech recognition engine accuracy weighs heavily on its training data. How many male vs female voices are in the training data? How big is the vocabulary of the training data? Did the training data have any speakers with a southern drawl? What about a Polish accent, a French accent, and a Spanish accent? Since these personal assistants are meant to be used by the public, is it going to know what an aileron is (aviation term)? As you can see, the number of variables can be huge, and the potential amount of data required is infinite. For example, if you tried an early version of speech recognition at the beginning of the 21st Century, many people found it did not understand female voices? The answer to "why?" is as simple as the original voice training data came from office co-workers who were asked to read a script into a microphone or a telephone. Those office workers were mostly male, so the female voice was not well represented in the original training data. Today, there have been new inventions and insertion of new techniques, such as deep learning, as well as a more diverse workplace, that have changed the way speech engines are trained, and a great deal of the issues with accents and background noise have gone away, and the error rate for speech recognition has come way down. By some measures, the most up to date speech recognition engines have an error rate of around 5%, which, in theory, is the same average error rate for a human listing to someone speak.

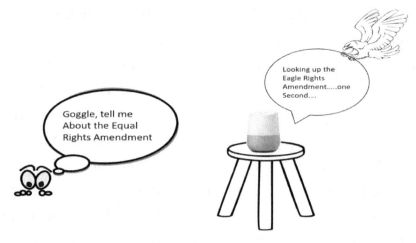

The next step in the journey into responding to your utterance is to figure out the intent of what you said. Today, to make the process of determining intent easier, all of the intents that a personal assistant can handle are pre-programmed into the assistant. That's right, the assistant is not taking your utterance and looking at the whole world of data and trying to figure out where your answer may lie. That would be something called a General Intelligence, which we will talk about a bit further ahead. There are a finite number of intents that it can handle. It can, for example, figure out that you are asking about the weather, and, once it does that, it looks in the text to see if you named a specific place, city, zip code, or country that is attached to your weather request. If not, it assumes you want the weather for the location stated in your profile. The fulfillment of that intent is also pre-programmed to go to a connected weather reporting service, then grab the information for the location and date you requested.

Here is an extremely small sample of intents that probably exist in your personal assistant

Weather – go to weather.com and get the weather forecast for the location and date in the utterance

Calendar – go to the calendar for the registered profile and read off today's events

Turn on/off Lights – send a command to the pre-registered light location mentioned and change the status of the bulb to the requested status (on/off)

Sports – go to sports.com and retrieve today's highlights

Ok, so we have four intents. Let's assume that there are no more intents in our assistant. It's pretty small, but it suits our purposes for demonstrating how these assistants work. Now you say an utterance like "What's on my schedule today?" The AI goes through each potential intent with the hypothesis, "this intent is what the utterance was about". Let's say that the AI engine comes back with the following:

Weather – 2% confidence that the utterance was about weather

Calendar – 76% confidence that the utterance was about calendar

Lights – 1% confidence that the utterance was about lights

Sports - 1% confidence that the utterance was about sports

Based on these results, the assistant is going to execute the weather program and look in the utterance for location and date information. Let's take a look at this same scenario again, using the utterance "What is Thomas Jefferson's birthday?" Our intent confidence scores may look something like this:

Weather – 2% confidence that the utterance was about weather

Calendar – 2% confidence that the utterance was about calendar

Lights – 1% confidence that the utterance was about lights

Sports - 1% confidence that the utterance was about sports

Here, no existing intent confidence score was greater than 5%, so the chances are, according to our AI engine, that no existing intent will be an appropriate response for the given utterance. The response will probably be something like "I'm not programmed to respond to that". Let's do one more example. Our utterance is "What was the score of the Cardinals game?"

Weather – 2% confidence that the utterance was about weather

Calendar – 2% confidence that the utterance was about calendar

Lights – 1% confidence that the utterance was about lights

Sports - 86% confidence that the utterance was about sports

Ok, the engine determined, correctly, that odds are you were asking about sports, so it executes the sports fulfillment routine, which is to go to sports.com and report the sports highlights for the day. The results of the Cardinals game may, or may not, be included in that report. Because there is no intent that specifically looks for something like "what was the results of the xxx game", with xxx representing the name of the sports team, there is no routine to go get that specific game result. Of course, as a frustrated user, you are asking" why don't they just add it?", and the answer is that they are adding new intents every day. They get thousands of requests asking for the addition of new intents and the programming that will respond appropriately to the intent. Originally, there were hundreds of intents covered. Now there are thousands of intents covered. Different devices have different intents, but they all tend to share the most common intents. If you use a personal assistant today, how many different intents are you using? Probably not more than 10 intents that you use on a regular basis. According to Amazon, the most common intents used by Alexa users are:

1. Set a timer
2. Play a song
3. Read the news
4. Control smart lights
5. Add item to shopping list
6. Connect to a paid music service

If you said, "add Clorox to my list", which of the 6 intents do you think would have the highest confidence score that it (the intent) was the most likely intent to fulfill your request. The fact that you said the word list would definitely add weight to choosing number five. And then if you look at the attributes of Clorox, you would find that it is a cleaning item usually found in a supermarket. That would add confidence to number 5 being the right intent to fire. There's no magic here. AI is all about intelligent guessing using weights and balances. If you were to figure out which of the six listed intents was the most likely to resemble what the user asked, you would go through the same steps, in microseconds. The computing device can go through those steps in microseconds, as well.

GENERAL INTELLIGENCE

Today the AI community thinks in terms of "Artificial Narrow Intelligence" (ANI), Artificial General Intelligence"(AGI), and Artificial Superintelligence(ASI). ANI is essentially all the AI we enjoy today. ANI can't accomplish many things that humans can, because ANI can't intuit, can't sense, and can't have what we call human emotions. Artificial General Intelligence (AGI) is the next step of AI research, and it has yet to been achieved. Right now, all commercial conversational AI engines are ANI, and are intent based, meaning they are pre-programmed to answer a certain finite set of questions. If, for example, you asked your car AI how to change a tire, it would be able to answer only because someone wrote that the intent "change a tire" should be recognized and answered with the content defined as the answer. Now let's pretend that we had an AI engine where all I needed to do was dump the entire owner's manual into my AI engine, without any pre-programmed intents, and you asked how to change a tire. If we had a general intelligence engine, it would learn from the manual, read through the instruction manual and only pick out the relevant information, and feed it back to you in an intelligent, conversational format. Likewise, you could dump the full contents of the World Encyclopedia into your general intelligence engine, and ask it anything you liked, in any way you liked, then it would understand the intent of your question, and extract the answer from the thousands of pages of content from the encyclopedias. Why is this so difficult? Certainly, humans can and do achieve this kind of intelligence every day. We, as humans, know how to determine an intent from whole cloth. A computer can't do that, as of today, without a list of inclusive intents. A computer can do a great job of figuring out which intent, out of a finite number of intents, which one most likely covers your question, but it can't do it without that head start. Artificial General Intelligence (AGI) is defined as an artificial intelligence that can perform any intellectual task that a human can perform. Taking that beyond AGI, a "strong AI" is defined as an AGI that has achieved consciousness. In abstract, Artificial General Intelligence simulates the human mind, while Strong AI IS a mind. The idea of creating, on a computer, an AI that has achieved consciousness is a bit too far into the weeds for this book to cover in depth but suffice to say that this is the end game for most AI scientist, who believe they will achieve this goal in their lifetime.

Already, autonomic cars, cars that drive themselves, are being programmed to simulate applied ethics. What should the computer do, for example, if the car it is driving comes into a traffic situation where the only two options are to drive into an occupied car, or run over a pedestrian crossing the road? How does a computer decide, if it has no consciousness, and no moral aptitude? This whole field of applied ethics in AI engines will take decades to figure out, and some say we are at least decades away from computers that can achieve consciousness. Others that are well known in the industry also say that the technology, as it exists today, will never achieve the level of General Intelligence. If we can never achieve AGI, then we definitely will never achieve Artificial Superintelligence. If you think about AGI making a machine equal to the ability of a human, then Artificial Superintelligence is making a machine that can accomplish things that no human could ever do. To get to any of these pivotal points in our future, there are still multiple inventions ahead of us that will be a quantum leap into the next stage of AI. It's ironic that I used the adverb "quantum" to describe the size of the leap yet to come. Indeed, the technology that may lead to this giant-sized leap, may be the quantum computer. Just like "hyper-speed" travel in space as described by multiple TV shows, quantum computers are a futuristic given in the TV world of the future. So, let's describe exactly what the ideas are behind quantum computers and why they may change the world.

We've all heard that today's computers are a bunch of 0s and 1s. That's correct. At its base level, today's computers do everything by turning on and off an electrical charge in tiny transistors that represent binary digits (bits). While the amount of the charge may differ between devices, the transistor that is more charged is considered a 1 and the less charged transistor is considered a 0. To confuse things, we call a group of bits a byte. All those bytes can be used as temporary or permanent storage. The storage isn't really permanent, because hard drives fail, and all of those bits and bytes go away. For those of you who have a computer, or phone, or tablet that is labelled 4GB of random–access memory (RAM), and 64GB of storage, that means that the temporary storage used by the computer that normally goes away when you turn the device off, is the 4GB. The 64GB represents more permanent storage where things don't go away when you turn off the device.

It's important to repeat that all of these devices are based on the principle that a single binary unit can temporarily hold the value of either 1 or 0. Despite the hype and what you may have heard, at the writing of this book, you cannot look at, buy, or demo a quantum computer. You can run simulations on powerful conventional computers, and there is an enormous amount of money being spent by the largest companies in the world, and the smallest startups, on Quantum Computing, but, as of today, there is no quantum computer.

Trying to describe a quantum computer in conventional computer terms is awkward, but a necessity for our purposes. Instead of those bits and bytes, a quantum computer is based on quantum bits, or qubits. Now here is where it gets funky. If you've ever watched Big Bang Theory, you've heard the terms Schrodinger's Cat, and, perhaps, quantum entanglement. Schrodinger's Cat is a thought experiment about the ability of a cat to exist in multiple states at the same time. The idea behind a quantum computer is that a qubit can exist in either state, at the same time, and, with quantum entanglement, a qubit could change its value, as well as the value of an entangled qubit at the same time. Don't worry if this sounds like gobbledygook. It is! The big problem with quantum computing is that these qubits are incredibly difficult to keep. They require incredible temperatures and magnets and the size of the quantum computer at IBM in Yorktown Heights fills a specially designed room full of very special equipment. If you had just 50 stable, error-free qubits that you could control, you would have enough computing power to eclipse anything conventional computers, of any size, can do.

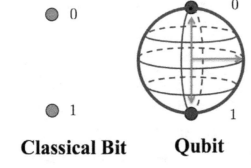

Classical Bit   **Qubit**

The promise of quantum computing is that, because if its incredible power and ability to do calculations impossible with current technology, it will change the face of what we can do, and what we can search through, to create impossibly powerful General AI technologies. WHEN? No one really knows, although because there is actually a prototype that can keep two atoms in an entangled state for up to two seconds, everyone thinks SOON. As a comparison, when, in the 1950s computer scientists were able to translate a few simple Russian sentences into meaningful English, scientists pronounced that the problem of human translation would be solved in the next five years. There are several really great quotes about predictions. My favorite is from Lao Tzu, *6th Century BC Chinese Poet who said "Those who have knowledge, don't predict. Those who predict, don't have knowledge. "*

MACHINE TRANSLATION

Machine Translation (MT), as demonstrated by Google Translate, Systran, SDL, and several other companies, is an AI solution that takes a content in one language, and outputs that content in a target language. For example, you may see a tag that says "translate me" next to a German website on a computer running an English language operating system. If you click on "translate me", an MT engine will take that German worded website, starting with the homepage, and translate the textual content, and then form a new webpage, replacing the English content with the German content. The translation will not be word for word, which would be almost incomprehensible, but it will translate segments that are seen as a single thought, such as sentences, or phrases. The result will not be perfect, and, in fact, may read as total gibberish. The intent of MT is to give the reader of a language that they do not understand, a gist of the content so that they can understand what the content was about. As someone who has built, sold, and marketed MT solutions for over 30 years, one of my biggest frustrations are people that speak two or more languages, using an MT engine to test how good the output is. Unfortunately, these individuals can't really get the value proposition of an MT engine. They can critique the wrong choice of words or the wrong gender or tense of a verb, but they can't really get the idea,

because they don't have a problem understanding the source or the target. Now, get a person who speaks no English at all, and show them an MTed English website in their native language, and they will tell you how successful the translation is.

As mentioned in a previous chapter, the first real rush to invest and perfect MT came in the late 50s when the US government and IBM came together to try to translate Russian messages. This was at the height of the cold war, and so the idea of not waiting days for overworked Russian translators was an appealing proposition. At first, scientists looked at the MT problem as a decoding problem. They wanted to approach translation in the same way they approached breaking a secret code. It didn't take too long to discover that this approach was doomed to failure. You can't decode a French sentence into English. So next they decided to simply use a large bilingual dictionary and simply replace one word with the equivalent in the target language. That failed quickly as the concept of syntax, or the order of words, became a hurtle. Also, there are lots of words in one language that don't have a partner word in another language. As an extreme example, there is a language in Africa that has only the colors black and white. As a syntax example, in the Spanish language, all of the adverbs go after the verb, while in English they go before the verb. Then there is the issue of ambiguous words, that have multiple senses. English is a highly ambiguous language, where lots of words are spelled the same way, but have very different meaning. "Can" can be a verb, or a noun. So can "crack". And with idioms, the verb "crack" can mean to tell, like in a joke, or to break something apart. So how does one account for all of these problems when translating from English to another language? Early MT systems were rule based, and they would try to map out the parts of speech for a sentence so that they could sew the words back together in a target language. Let's take a look at the simple sentence "The cow jumped over the moon." First, we diagram the sentence and assign parts of speech.

"The"   "cow" "jumped" "over"   "the"   " moon"
article   subject main verb adverb   article   object

Next, we would check through the rules database and see if there are any exceptions for sentences where the main verb is "to jump", the subject of the verb is "cow", and the object is "moon". There aren't any specific rules since this is a normally behaving sequence of words, so we go get the equivalent words in the target language, make sure all of the tenses are copied, and then rearrange the word order based on the syntax rules of the target language. The quality of the translations were based on the number of rules to cover ambiguous scenarios. As rule bases grew larger and larger, the systems got slower and slower, even as computing power got greater every year. MT scientists realized that this was just a stop-gap measure and that they had pretty much hit a quality ceiling, because everything was based on writing more and more rules, which is unsustainable.

When Google got into the game, with Google Translate, they were using a very new method called statistical MT. They were no longer mapping the source sentences syntactically and semantically. Instead, they were using a large body of parallel translations to guess, statistically, the likelihood of the accuracy of n best translations. In a precursor to what would eventually be called deep learning, they were using huge corpus of translations to find large segments that had a high confidence of being the same as the source segments, much like the Rosetta Stone.

Citation: Kevin Knight and Philipp Koehn, *What's New in Statistical Machine Translation*

In the reference diagram above, what you are seeing is an example of how, in a large corpus of content that is equal, but in French and English, the statistical engine has picked up that "the house" and "la maison" seem to be equal. So, whenever the translation engine comes across the phrase "the house", it can translate it into "la maison".

Now, MT has moved to the neural net/deep learning phase of technology. As we saw in an earlier chapter, with neural nets we might take a phrase of a sentence in the source language, and then search through the corpus in the target language for a phrase with a high confidence of meaning the same thing. Thus, with neural net based MT, we don't have large bi-directional dictionaries, because we don't translate at the word level. We also don't have to worry that a source word may not have an equivalent in the target language because, again, we are looking for sentence fragments that have the same meaning, so words become less important. As to when we should expect a little earbud that will automatically translate perfectly all other languages into our native language, I would suggest not until we have perfected an artificial general intelligence. Computers need to be able to understand idiomatic expressions, sarcasm, comedy, and more that are only human attributes, for now.

BIOMETRICS

The concept of using your voice, or your fingerprint, or your iris as a means of identification is a field called biometrics. Today, we see finger print biometrics on just about every mobile phone. We also see face print biometrics, with the idea being that the camera can scan your face to determine if it "looks" like you. The idea behind all of these biometric identifiers is to locate distinguishing characteristics in the feature being matched. For example, face biometrics is not about comparing a picture of you to live, in person you. When the software scans your face, it is finding certain mandatory points,

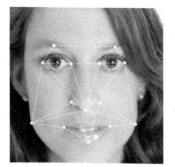 such as where your eyes are, where your nose is, and then finding associated points, and measuring the distance between those points. You can wear a disguise, but these facial features don't move with a disguise. You can grow a beard, or a mustache, but, again, these points don't change. Can you fool face biometrics with a picture of the enrolled person instead of the real live thing? Makers of

biometric software put proprietary "check for life" modules in their software to look for things that would indicate this is a live experience, and not someone trying to fool the biometric engine. For facial recognition, a lot of developers use technology that looks for eye blinking to ensure that they are matching against a live person and not a picture.

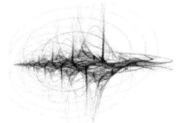

Voice biometrics, like other forms of biometrics, finds distinct markers in your voiceprint. One new to the market voice biometrics engine claims to use over 400 different biomarkers, that is, voice markers that can be detected on a consistent basis, to make a match between a person's live voice, and their biometric enrollment. Current thought is that matching discreet patterns on a person's iris is the most accurate form of biometric identification, and the hardest to spoof, since it requires blood running through it. There are lots of YouTube™ entries showing you how to lift a fingerprint off of a glass and use that to fool a simple fingerprint matching system. You can sort of see how augmented reality will eventually be able to deceive facial recognition systems. One thing is sure, for as long as there are developers creating new ways of using biometric markers to identify people, there will be people figuring out how to defeat the system.

SELF DRIVING CARS

So what's the deal with self-driving cars? Can cars really be trusted to drive themselves? How does that work? What does it mean when you talk about what the car "sees". There's already been accidents reported, and one fatality around self-driving cars. People are definitely divided on this, and since very few people really understand how self-driving cars work, we can safely state that most of the divide is based on emotion, not fact. Let's look at the facts. First of all, how can a car see? Well, there are tiny cameras placed all over the car pointing in all directions. To figure out why that matters, let's go back to our rose detection engine. Remember how the AI engine could look at a flower and determine if it was a picture of a rose? Now imagine that the engine is trained to determine if the picture is a picture of a person. And it's also trained to determine if it is a picture of a STOP sign, or a YIELD sign, etc. You get the idea. All of these cameras show the engine what is around the car in 360 degrees, and the engine is trained on detecting with high confidence hundreds, if not thousands if "things" that are important to driving. That is a somewhat simplified view, but it works for our discussion. It can also determine if something is moving, and by judging movement over time, it can determine the rate of speed of the object, as well.

Even if it can see, and recognize everything in a 360-degree view, how can it make judgement decisions. Well that is where the whole safety and ethics questions begin.

The "Trolley problem" is a thought experiment exploring ethics. In it, you, dear reader, are stationed at a switch which controls which of two directions a runaway trolley will take. In one direction there are five people tied to the railroad tracks, and on the other direction, there is one person tied to the railroad tracks. In some variations of the experiment, the single person is a child, which potentially adds a new dimension to the experiment. If you do nothing, then the five people tied to the tracks perish, whereas, if you pull the switch, the single person on the other tracks will perish.

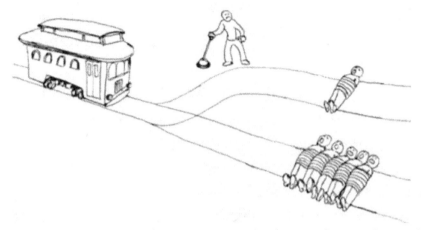

If it were a simple mathematical problem, then the choice would be obvious, but the experiment is more difficult than that. If you do nothing, then one might say that nature takes its course, while if you pull the lever, you are actively killing the single person. Thus, the paradox. To extend that paradox, what is the AI driven car to do? For the car, it is not an ethical question, as computers don't have ethics. What computers have is rules. And those rules are coded by developers. If an AI driven car were faced with a dilemma similar to the trolley problem, how is it supposed to react? Who makes that decision, as it has to have a programmed response. For the AI is it simply a math problem? 5 vs 1? Or a school bus vs a sedan?

These are the kinds of questions that are stumping the auto industry with AI driven cars.

In 1950, in a book called "I, Robot", the great science fiction writer Isaac Asimov laid out the three principle rules to keep our AIs from killing us.

1) A robot may not injure a human being or, through inaction, allow a human being to come to harm.

2) A robot must obey orders given to it by human beings except where such orders would conflict with the First Law.

3) A robot must protect its own existence as long as such protection does not conflict with the First or Second Law.

As we see in the trolley problem, it isn't that hard to come up with a paradox that shreds these rules. Even in a narrow AI world, where computers only do what we program them to do, where there is no free will for the AI, paradoxes like the Trolley Problem abound and create lots of discussions on AI ethics. Just because we have no idea when we will be able to create a General AI, there is no reason to not work on the issues we will face in our future. Which brings up the next question.

IS MY AI GOING TO KILL ME?

Probably not. And I say probably not just to scare you a little bit. Maybe a better answer is "It depends". If you read a lot of news, you probably know that famous thinkers such as Stephen Hawking, and Elon Musk, have talked about an AI Apocalypse, where AI robots become the masters, and humans become the slaves. Scary stuff and great fodder for books and movies. You also have luminaries such as Bill Gates saying we shouldn't fear AI, we should control it. Like any scientific advance, if it is misused, it can hurt you. For example, if you're using AI to drive your car while you sit in the back seat drinking coffee and reading a book, then, yes, your AI might kill you. But that statement may be moot in another decade. Like just about everything in our environment today, if you use it in ways it was not meant to be used, then it can be dangerous. If you put that dry-cleaning bag over your head (don't do it), even though there is a warning not to do that, then you may end up dead, because you used the bag in a way not intended. It's not the AI that is dangerous, it's you! Folks like Elon Musk are so worried about AI killing us that they have co-founded nonprofits, like OpenAI to study how best to control and monitor AI to make sure it's not destroying mankind in some insidious way. Remember, we aren't even close to a general artificial intelligence, and we can't even agree on what gives us our human qualities so that we would know when we have created an AGI. Of course, there are ways that bad computer code could do serious damage without the need for a runaway AI system. Everything we do seems to be wrapped in computer code now, including our military procedures, our nuclear arsenal, and more. Accidents caused by bad code could happen in these environments, but there are supposed to be mitigations to mitigations to prevent that kind of thing from happening. But, overall, if we use technology the way it was intended to be used and keep the dry-cleaning bag away from our heads, then I think we'll be in pretty good shape. However, like the recent self-driving car accident that killed the driver, there will be artificial normal intelligence (ANI) based accidents which will make headlines. And there are AI based events that can hurt you in ways not physical. Take the case of a six-year-old girl in Dallas who asked her Alexa™ device if it would get her a dollhouse, which it conveniently did, along with four pounds of sugar cookies. The story doesn't end there, as the story was picked up by a local morning TV show in San Diego, where the morning host merely said "I love the little girl saying 'Alexa, order me a dollhouse'". Of course, those listening households with nearby Alexa devices found that they, too, were the proud new owners of a dollhouse. There are mitigations to stop things like that from happening.   In the case of Alexa, you can set the purchase option to require verification before the order is placed.   It's just a matter of making sure that, as the human, you take advantage of efforts by the manufacturer to mitigate or stop mistakes from happening.

HOW DO I GET THERE FROM HERE?

Perhaps one of the most used, but least talked about use of AI in everyday life is the ability of programs like Waze and Apple Maps to get us from point A to point B with the fastest route. To understand how this works, let's look at the bits and pieces that it needs to know in order to give you the right answer. To start with, these engines have a complete map of their covered areas, and I do mean complete. Thanks to a combination of those little cars with cameras mounted on top, and mapping services, and crowdsourcing, these mapping services know every alley and every one-way street in your town. The question is, how do they find the fastest route? Just imagine that the map of your city as a maze, with lots of potential ways of getting from point A to point B, but only one best route from point A

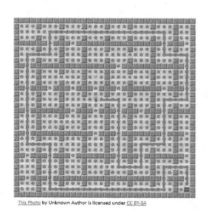

to point B. The shortest route is not necessarily the complete route with the shortest distance between the two points. If we take time into consideration, then the best and shortest route is the route that gets us from point A to point B in the least amount of time. So how do these apps know what the traffic is, and the average speed per car? Two ways. One way, which is used by Waze, lets users give immediate feedback to the crowd on accidents, speed traps, etc. Also, there are probably other drivers using the same app that are on these roads, and your mobile phone has the ability, built in, to report back on what your average speed is. With almost everyone driving having a mobile phone in their automobiles, the amount of data that these engines can collect in real time is staggering. Now, of course, it still has to solve the maze. It has to find every route from A to B that is possible, and then compute the time it takes for each route, and then show you the fastest route. Many of these solutions will allow you to reject routes with tolls, or interstate highways, and offer alternative routes. The thing about Neural Nets is that they can crack mazes in seconds, because they can literally start multiple route approaches simultaneously. When you look at how it solves the maze problem, it is not elegant, it is brute force, but it works. Each starting point proceeds to all possible routes. Routes that get shut down are excluded, and routes that make it all the way from A to B are included and calculated for total time/distance. Of course, not all maps are totally accurate, nor kept up to date, so when your favorite directions app tries to tell you to turn left coming out of the airport car rental garage, and there is no left turn available, you just have to grit your teeth, turn right, and wait for the app to say "recalculating location".

Here I will ask, and then answer some quick questions about AI that don't need their own chapter to keep you informed.

Q: What is Python?

A: A great way to tell someone who really understands AI from the pretenders is to ask them "are you doing everything in Python?" If they don't quickly answer "of course", then you can assume something is amiss. What is python, besides a snake that is over-populating the Florida Everglades? It is a programming language, like C# or Java, or, for those from an earlier generation, Cobol, that is used almost exclusively for building AI applications. Conceived of in the 1980s, it was fully implemented by Guido van Rossum in the Netherlands, in 1989. He named the programming language after "Monty Python's Flying Circus", which was a BBC comedy series from the 70s. Today, everyone from Google to IBM uses python as the premium programming language for AI solutions.

Q: Will AI take all of our jobs?

A: No, just most of them. Kidding. AI will definitely replace some repetitive jobs, such as jobs robots on an assembly line can do faster, cheaper, and non-stop. Simple tasks such as taking a food order or answering phone calls can be handled by conversational AI solutions with excellent results today. On the other hand, anyone can start a new company with a tiny investment today by renting cloud computing, software, and other technologies on a consumption basis, so there are many new higher paying jobs today because AI and technology in general.

Q: Is AI responsible for hacking into our lives?

A: No. Most successful hacks are still achieved by taking advantage of the human condition. As an example, one of the companies that I've worked for sent me a note that my social security number had been exposed by a hack. But the hack was that someone emailed an individual claiming to be the head of the company asking for a list of all employees, and the person responded. So called "social hacking" is the primary culprit in most hacks. Most of this type of hacking centers around getting you to click on a link that will implant a virus on your computer. You've probably already received emails that seem to be from a known friend that implores you to click on a link to see something important. If the email is suspicious, it is easy enough to email the person (don't hit reply, start a new email), and ask if they sent it.

Q: Can AI write software code?

A: Yes, but don't be too impressed. Code generators have been around for years and are basically templates that get filled in by some slot filling variables. I can tell a code generator to generate the C# code to get the name, address, zip code, and phone number on a form, and it can generate that code pretty quickly, but only because someone in advance wrote a template that says "when you want to get a phone number, insert this code." When we get to a working artificial general intelligence, then it should be possible to simply describe what an application should do, and have an AI write the code. See the next chapter on the Singularity.

Q: Is AI changing the face of warfare?

A: Absolutely. One thing that AI does extremely well is identify objects. With the correct training, AI is able to use facial recognition to identify a specific individual, just like it is able to find a specific building or mapped area. With this kind of advanced targeting capability, along with advances in drones of all sizes, we have the ability to search and destroy without putting any soldiers on the field of battle, or in the air. It is not hard to imagine where technology may lead us in the near future.

There is a lot of content on the internet about how AI can be used in evil ways and whether or not we are destroying ourselves. While that topic is literally the subject of millions of pages, I've tried to summarize in one chapter.

WHAT IS THE SINGULARITY?

Perhaps a better question is "what is 'A' singularity?" Looking at an English dictionary, it has two distinct meetings. The first meaning is state, fact, quality, or condition of being singular, such as in the sentence "I enjoy the singularity of every snowflake". Every snowflake has a unique pattern, like fingerprints, so each snowflake is a singular event. The other meaning is a point at which a function takes an infinite value, especially in space-time when matter is infinitely dense, as at the center of a black hole. It gets used both ways, but the way that the movies treat the term is probably the most common. **Originally popularized by science fiction writer Vernor Vinge, a singularity is considered a point in time in human evolution where everything changes so dramatically that nothing we learned in the past has any relevance. Most people associate this event with the creation of an artificial super intelligence, because an ASI would be able to change all of the rules of how we live and what we do each day.**

"We are on the edge of change comparable to the rise of human life on Earth, the precise cause of this change is the imminent creation by technology of entities with greater than human intelligence."
Vernor Vinge, 1993

Even though movies and TV shows try to imagine the singularity, if it is something that is currently beyond our comprehension, we can't really describe it, or it wouldn't be the singularity. One could argue that, looking back in time, the industrial revolution was a singularity. Think of someone from the early 18th century, say, 1710, in the US, waking up today. They wouldn't understand much about how we live our everyday lives. Our homes, our work, even our play, would be totally outside of anything they know. They wouldn't understand how we communicate, or even how we recreate. Perhaps the invention of the internet was also a singularity. Both of these events changed forever the way we lived on earth. They both dramatically changed the workforce, the environment, the way we play, and the way we live. If there were a super intelligence, think of the way technologies like augmented and virtual reality could change the way we live. Wouldn't that create a singularity? Likewise, if we had complete control over the entire human genome, which a super intelligence would be able to achieve, think of how humans would evolve, and how rapidly. Of course, this is all speculation, but the idea of a singularity will continue to be a focus of books, movies, and tv shows for decades to come. There may even be a singularity in our lifetimes!

Here's my final summary on AI as it stands today. Right now, it is all very clever programming and architecture that allows us to do cool things that used to take a lot more time and effort. It always has an error rate, and most people don't expect or understand that, so they are pretty frustrated when the computer doesn't do what they told it to do. Some people yell at it, sing to it, and even try to be nice to it, but let's face it, it's just software sitting on some hardware. It doesn't understand your frustration or feel your pain. It doesn't get scared, and it doesn't get tired. It just responds to what it is asked to do, sometimes correctly, and sometimes not correctly. It will always fail, some of the time. If you keep that in mind, and keep your expectations in check, than you and AI can probably live a   healthy   life   together.

ABOUT THE AUTHOR

Brian Garr has spent over 30 years helping to build the computer industry as a CEO, COO, CRO, and CTO of various software startups, primarily in the artificial intelligence space, as well as a decade at IBM working on speech recognition and machine translation. He is considered a subject matter expert on AI and has spoken around the world on the topic. In 1998 he was awarded the Smithsonian Institutes' "Heroes in Technology" award for his work in Machine Translation. He has published multiple white papers and documents on AI, as well as a chapter on Machine Translation in an AI textbook often used in college level courses. He has acted as a professional witness for AI specific legal cases. He lives in Boca Raton, Florida with his wife, Lisa, and his English Bull Terrier, Brandy.